Shots Fired at Fort Sumter
Civil War Breaks Out!

Wendy Vierow

The Rosen Publishing Group's
PowerKids Press™
New York

For Chris

Published in 2004 by The Rosen Publishing Group, Inc.
29 East 21st Street, New York, NY 10010

First Edition

Editor: Frances E. Ruffin

Book Design: Michael de Guzman

Photo Credits: Cover (inset photo), pp. 5, 7, 9 (top), 12, 14, 17, 20, 21 Library of Congress, Prints and Photographs Division; Cover (rifle) Photo by Peter Latner, Minnesota Historical Society; (hats) Cindy Reiman; p. 8 © National Portrait Gallery, Smithsonian Institution/Art Resource; p. 9 (bottom) John Rankin House, Small Picture Collection, Ohio Historical Society; p. 11 Library of Congress, Manuscript Division; p. 13 Print Collection, Miriam and Ira D. Wallach Division of Art, Prints and Photographs Division, The New York Public Library, Astor, Lenox and Tilden Foundations; p. 15 Still Picture Branch, National Archives and Records Administration; p. 19 Library of Congress, Maps Division.

Vierow, Wendy.
Shots fired at Fort Sumter : Civil War breaks out / by Wendy Vierow.—1st ed.
   p. cm. — (Headlines from history)
Includes bibliographical references and index.
Summary: Describes the events leading up to South Carolina's secession from the Union and the firing on Fort Sumter that led to the beginning of the Civil War.
 ISBN 0-8239-6220-2 (lib. bdg.)
1. Fort Sumter (Charleston, S.C.)—Siege, 1861—Juvenile literature. 2. Charleston (S.C.)—History—Civil War, 1861–1865—Juvenile literature. 3. United States—History—Civil War, 1861–1865—Causes—Juvenile literature. [1. Fort Sumter (Charleston, S.C.)—Siege, 1861. 2. United States—History—Civil War, 1861–1865—Causes.] I. Title. II. Series.
 E471.1 .V54 2003
 973.7'11—dc21

2001005468

Manufactured in the United States of America

CONTENTS

Fort Sumter Is Built in Charleston

Charleston Harbor is in Charleston, South Carolina. It is an important port where ships bring goods in and out of the city of Charleston.

In the 1700s, American colonists built a fort out of sand, wood, and earth to protect Charleston Harbor from the British during the **American Revolution**. Later the U.S. Army decided to build other forts to protect Charleston Harbor. In 1827, U.S. Army engineers made plans to build a strong, brick fort. Work began on the fort two years later.

The new fort had five sides, and it was two stories high. Guns were added to protect Charleston Harbor. Workers built three

This is a painting of Charleston Harbor in Charleston, South Carolina. It is the place where, in April 1861, the Civil War began.

buildings inside the fort so that soldiers could live there.

In December 1860, the fort, called Fort Sumter, was still not finished. Little did anyone know that the first shots of the Civil War would be fired there a few months later.

States Argue over Slavery

People have different opinions about why the Civil War started. Many agree that the causes of the war came from disagreements about the practice of **slavery** in the United States.

Most slaves came from Africa. They were forced to work long hours without pay. Slaves were not American citizens and had no rights. They could be bought and sold. They could be separated from their families. Many slaves tried to run away. They wanted to be free.

Over time people who lived in the Northern part of the United States began to think that slavery was wrong. They made laws against slavery. Southern leaders argued that the South needed the free labor of slaves to run **plantations**, or big

This painting shows Senator Henry Clay from Kentucky speaking before Congress about the issue of slavery.

farms. Leaders of Northern and Southern states argued in Congress about slavery.

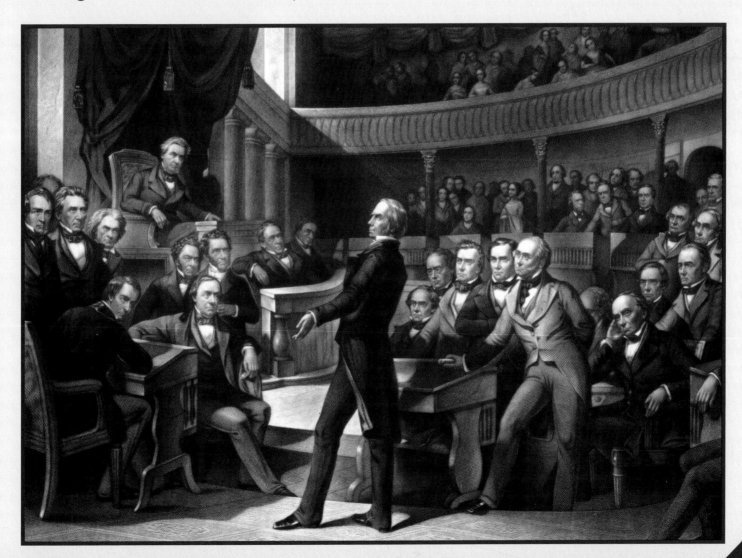

Abolitionists Anger Southerners

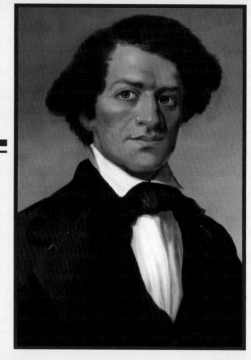

There were people who worked to end slavery. They were called **abolitionists**. They believed that slavery should be against the law. Abolitionists included both white and black people. Abolitionist Frederick Douglass, who was once a slave, spoke out against slavery.

Some abolitionists worked on the **Underground Railroad**. The Underground Railroad was a chain of people who helped slaves escape to Canada and to safe places in the United States. The law stated that all escaped slaves had to be returned to their owners. Abolitionists who helped slaves escape broke the law

The steps in this photo lead to an Underground Railroad location where slaves were hidden on their travels to freedom in the North.

Frederick Douglass, a former slave, spoke out and wrote books against the practice of slavery.

Harriet Tubman led slaves to freedom on the Underground Railroad.

and could be sent to jail. They were willing to take this risk because they felt so strongly that slavery was wrong.

Abolitionist Harriet Tubman was a slave who escaped on the Underground Railroad. Once she had escaped, she made many dangerous trips in the South and in the North to help slaves escape. Many plantation owners offered rewards to anyone who could catch her, but no one ever did.

Many Southerners were angry at abolitionists for helping slaves. The issue of slavery divided the North and the South more each day.

Abraham Lincoln Is Elected President

In November 1860, many people campaigned for the presidency of the United States. Some people running for president thought that slavery should be allowed. Others thought that slavery should be against the law.

One person who ran for president was Abraham Lincoln. He once said, "If slavery is not wrong, then nothing is wrong. I cannot remember when I did not so think and feel."

Lincoln thought that slavery should not be allowed in any new states joining the United States. Because of his stand on this issue, leaders in South Carolina threatened to **secede** from, or

There were many photographs taken of President Abraham Lincoln. Most showed him with a beard, but this is an earlier photo of him without a beard.

leave, the **Union** if Lincoln were elected. More than anything, Lincoln wanted to make sure that no states left the United States.

Abraham Lincoln won the November election. He would become president in March 1861. His election angered many people in the South.

The Confederacy Is Born

![Charleston Mercury Extra announcing the Union is Dissolved]

CHARLESTON

MERCURY

EXTRA:

Passed unanimously at 1.15 o'clock, P. M., December 20th, 1860.

AN ORDINANCE

To dissolve the Union between the State of South Carolina and other States united with her under the compact entitled "The Constitution of the United States of America."

We, the People of the State of South Carolina, in Convention assembled, do declare and ordain, and it is hereby declared and ordained,

That the Ordinance adopted by us in Convention, on the twenty-third day of May, in the year of our Lord one thousand seven hundred and eighty-eight, whereby the Constitution of the United States of America was ratified, and also, all Acts and parts of Acts of the General Assembly of this State, ratifying amendments of the said Constitution, are hereby repealed; and that the union now subsisting between South Carolina and other States, under the name of "The United States of America," is hereby dissolved.

THE

UNION

IS

DISSOLVED!

People in the South were upset that Lincoln was elected the country's new president. They did not like Lincoln's view that new states should not be allowed to have slavery. Many Southerners believed in **states' rights**. They thought that the people of each state should be given the right to decide whether slavery should be allowed in their state.

 The December 20, 1860 Charleston Mercury announced the secession of Southern states.

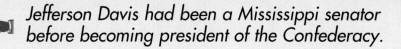

Jefferson Davis had been a Mississippi senator before becoming president of the Confederacy.

After Lincoln was elected president, South Carolina carried out its threat to leave the United States. In December 1860, South Carolina seceded from the United States. It was soon followed by five other states. These were Mississippi, Florida, Alabama, Georgia, and Louisiana. Leaders of the six states met and created their own country, the **Confederate States of America**, or the **Confederacy**. They declared independence from the United States. They made their own **constitution**. They elected Jefferson Davis, a former U.S. senator from Mississippi, as their president. Texas soon left the Union and joined the Confederacy.

13

The Confederacy Surrounds Fort Sumter

The Confederacy began to take control of U.S. property in the South. This included post offices, forts, and other buildings. **Confederate** leaders said that this property was part of their country, the Confederate States of America.

To protect Fort Sumter in Charleston Harbor, Major Robert Anderson moved his troops there on December 26, 1860. He was in charge of protecting the fort for the United States. However,

Union major Robert Anderson was commander of Fort Sumter.

14

☞ *Confederate general Pierre Gustave Toutant Beauregard of Louisiana led the attack on Fort Sumter.*

Confederate troops wanted to take over Fort Sumter. They aimed their cannons at the fort but did not yet fire. President Abraham Lincoln took office in March 1861. Lincoln received a message from Anderson that U.S. soldiers would soon run out of food. They would have to surrender to the Confederates when food ran out. President Lincoln decided to send supply ships to the fort. President Jefferson Davis thought that the Confederacy should not let soldiers at Fort Sumter receive Union supplies. He told Confederate general Pierre Gustave Toutant Beauregard to demand the **surrender** of Fort Sumter.

The Confederacy Fires on Fort Sumter

On April 11, 1861, Confederate officers visited Fort Sumter and asked Major Anderson to surrender. Major Anderson refused to surrender unless his food ran out. The officers told Major Anderson that they would fire on the fort.

On April 12, 1861, General Beauregard ordered his troops to fire on Fort Sumter. Citizens from Charleston, South Carolina, gathered on their rooftops to watch the fight. Shells from Confederate cannons caused fires in the fort, but no one was injured or killed on either side. The fighting continued for 34 long hours. Major Anderson surrendered the next day. As his troops

This painting shows Fort Sumter under attack from Confederate cannons.

fired a final cannon salute, one Union soldier was killed by his own troops, and five were wounded.

The Confederacy had taken over the fort and had fired on the United States of America. The Civil War had begun, and the Confederacy had won the first battle.

More States Leave the Union

After the Union lost the fight at Fort Sumter, more states joined the Confederacy. The border states of Virginia, Arkansas, North Carolina, and Tennessee seceded from the Union. They were called border states because they lay on either side of the border between the North and the South.

Most people in the western part of Virginia did not want to join the Confederacy. They did not think that slavery was right. They chose to stay in the Union, and they decided to break away from Virginia. Later the people there formed the new state of West Virginia.

The states shown in purple represent the United States of America. The Confederate States of America are colored orange, and the border states are shown in brown.

Some border states allowed slavery but stayed in the Union. Kentucky, Missouri, Maryland, and Delaware were allowed to keep slavery in their states even though they stayed in the Union. If they had to give up their slaves, they probably would have become Confederate states. Lincoln needed those states to win the war.

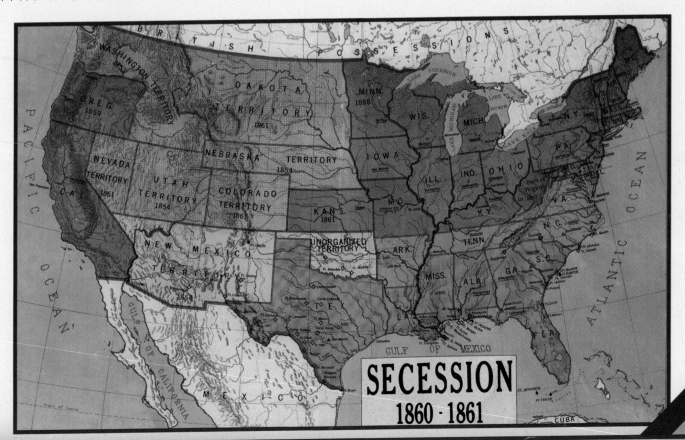

SECESSION
1860 - 1861

The Confederacy Against the Union

After the first shots of the Civil War were fired at Fort Sumter on April 12, 1861, both sides got ready for war. Many people on both sides thought that they would win the war easily and quickly.

The Confederacy had 11 states and nine million people, three and a half million of whom were slaves. Many Southern farmers could leave

👉 *Soldiers fighting for the Union had blue uniforms and were sometimes called the blues.*

home to fight because slaves kept the plantations running. Slaves were not allowed to fight for the Confederacy until the war was almost finished. Southern farmers who went to war knew how to fire guns and ride horses, unlike many Northerners, who lived in cities. The Union had more states and people than did the Confederacy. It had 23 states, six **territories**, and 22 million people. The Union also had many factories. Because of its factories, it had better supplies than did the Confederacy. Each side had its own advantages. Each side thought that it could win.

Confederate soldiers wore gray uniforms and were sometimes referred to as the grays.

Soldiers Join the Fight

Within a week after the fight at Fort Sumter, some free African American men formed a group in Pittsburgh, Pennsylvania, called the Hannibal Guards. Hannibal was a North African general in the third century B.C. The Hannibal Guards were ready to fight for the Union army, but black men would have to wait until 1863 for the law to let them become soldiers.

Many families had members who fought on different sides of the Civil War. President Lincoln and his wife, Mary Todd Lincoln, supported the Union, but Mary had three stepbrothers and a brother-in-law who fought for the Confederacy.

Men hurried to join the Confederate and the Union armies. They were afraid that the war would be finished before they could fight. Little did either side know that the war would last for four years. Finally, in 1865, the Union won the Civil War.

GLOSSARY

abolitionists (a-buh-LIH-shun-ists) People who worked to end slavery.

American Revolution (uh-MER-uh-ken reh-vuh-LOO-shun) Battles that soldiers from the American colonies fought against England for freedom.

Civil War (SIH-vul WOR) The war fought between the Northern and Southern states of America from 1861 to 1865.

Confederacy (kun-FEH-duh-reh-see) The Confederate states.

Confederate (kun-FEH-duh-ret) A person who fought for the South during the Civil War.

Confederate States of America (kun-FEH-duh-ret STAYTZ UV uh-MER-ih-kuh) A group of 11 southern states that declared themselves separate from the United States in 1860.

constitution (kahn-stih-TOO-shun) The basic rules by which a country or a state is governed.

plantations (plan-TAY-shunz) Very large farms. In the South, plantation crops were harvested by slaves.

secede (sih-SEED) To withdraw from a group or a country.

slavery (SLAY-vuh-ree) The system of one person "owning" another.

states' rights (STAYTS RYTS) When states believe that they, rather than the federal government, should decide on certain issues, such as slavery.

surrender (suh-REN-der) To give up.

territories (TEHR-ih-tor-eez) Parts of the United States that are not states.

Underground Railroad (UN-der-grownd RAYL-rohd) A chain of people who helped slaves to escape to Canada and other safe places in the United States.

Union (YOON-yun) The Northern states during the Civil War.

INDEX

PRIMARY SOURCES

Page 5: Fort Sumter—Peacetime. Print by Currier & Ives (1852–1907). Library of Congress. **Page 7**: The United States Senate. Engraving by P.F. Rothermel (1850). Library of Congress. **Page 8**: Frederick Douglass. Painting (1844). National Portrait Gallery, Smithsonian Institution. **Page 9** (bottom): Freedom Stairway. Ohio Historical Society, Small Picture Collection American Memory—The African American Experience in Ohio (1850–1920). **Page 9** (top): Harriet Tubman. Photograph by H.B. Lindsley. Library of Congress. **Page 11**: Abraham Lincoln. Photograph by Mathew Brady (1860). Library of Congress. **Page 12**: Secession announcement from the Charleston Mercury (1860). Library of Congress. **Page 13**: Jefferson Davis. Engraving by J. C. Buttre. New York Public Library. **Page 14**: Major Robert Anderson. Photograph by George Smith Cook (1861). Library of Congress, American Memory—Selected Civil War Photographs. **Page 15**: General Pierre Gustave Toutant Beauregard. Photograph by Mathew Brady Studio (1860–1865). National Archives and Records Administration. **Page 17**: Bombardment of Fort Sumter, Charleston Harbor. Print by Currier & Ives. Library of Congress. **Page 19**: Secession 1860–1861, by Albert Bushness Hart. Civil War Map. Library of Congress. **Page 20**: Portrait of a Federate Soldier. Photograph (1860–1865). Library of Congress. **Page 21**: Portrait of a Confederate Soldier. Photograph (1860–1865). Library of Congress.

WEB SITES

To learn more about Fort Sumter, check out this Web site:
http://library.thinkquest.org/3055/graphics/battles/fortsumter.html